Five Big Questions in Life
And how to answer them

Ched,

Thanks so much.
God bless!
Enjoy!

Wilder Publications, Inc.
PO Box 632
Floyd Va 24091

Copyright ©2012 by Miriam Pia

Cover © Can Stock Photo Inc. / librafoto

ISBN-13: 978-1-61720-864-5
ISBN-10: 1-61720-864-7

FIRST EDITION

10 9 8 7 6 5 4 3 2 1

Five Big Questions in Life
And how to answer them

by Miriam Pia
PD/MA offered by Middlesex University 1999
SUNY Brockport cum laude 1994

[introductory philosophy for a general audience]
* 'a trained philosopheress'

*the love of wisdom, and the purpose is to equip people to be able to practice philosophy using themselves, their own brains and feet with some guidance on how to do philosophy from this book.

Author's Credentials

2005: Writers Bureau—Certificate of Competence in Creative Writing

1999: Postgraduate Diploma—Middlesex University, Modern European Philosophy.

1994: Bachelor of Science cum laude, State University of New York at Brockport, Western Philosophy

1986: Regents High School Diploma, Syracuse NY

Acknowledgments

The professors who encouraged me, the divine inspiration that has made me persist in this, the God or gods that made me talented in this area—which caused me to do this for you all, all of you who read the work and benefit from it—especially those who help support me and my small family by actually buying a copy, the entire history of philosophy which has led us to this point and condition. To the muses and school teachers who made sure I became literate. Of course, supportive loved ones and invisible allies.

Table of Contents

Chapter 1: Introduction

What is philosophy? Translated literally from the Greek, it means "love of wisdom". It has been around for approximately 3000 years in the West. The world's first known, remembered philosopher is Confucious of China over 1000 years before remembered Greek philosophers.

Another simple way to understand what philosophy is to describe it: the subject that tries to answer some of the questions in life that are hardest to answer. Philosophy takes more effort to practice than it does to just think about. For adult readers, the most obvious way you have seen this is whenever you have taken a new job. The company often gives you a small flier. One paragraph of the flier gives you the philosophy. They give it to you with the Mission Statement and the Vision so that you understand core principles of the organization. The entire business functions daily—and its all in an effort to implement that little bit of philosophy. That's how much more there is to doing philosophy than there is to learning the theories.

There are a lot of trained professionals who practice philosophy and who clarify the theories involved. Whether done by amateurs or professionals, it is important work. Most cultures have a history of philosophy, which is a history of theories about fundamental truths and how to live one's life. Much of religion includes philosophy. Whenever there is a God or were gods closely associated with the philosophy, it is called theology. If it associated with a "mystery school" or the occult or paranormal then it is often referred to as theosophy or as metaphysics. When it shows up without a religious package it is normally just called philosophy, and is taught in the secular world.

Of the world's religions, the most famous for philosophy are the Catholics—just a few of them, such as Saint Thomas Aquinas. Thomas Aquinas looked at the ideas at the very root of Jesus Christ's teachings and then he compared them to the ideas put forward by some of the West's most powerful philosophers. We should point out—the other philosophers were not usually also Christians. Aquinas confronted Aristotle and Plato, and if anyone mostly understands, this is no simple feat. Also, during the time of Aquinas' life, there was a well known and specific system of intellectual and spiritual debate. The Summa Theologica—naturally originally written in Latin, was a giant work in which Aquinas worked through major arguments and made counter arguments to some of the most powerful 'other ideas' of his era. The Buddhists seem to always be talking about the philosophy of the mind and of the emotions and how to practice compassion. That is, the top Buddhists seem to emphasize this when writing or speaking in English for a nonBuddhist audience. Being part of that audience, I have no idea what its like for Tibetans who grew up Buddhists but I also don't know what its like to grow up a wealthy upper middle class Californian Buddhist. There are people that do.

Those are not the only philosophers in the world. Most readers have at least heard of Confucius. There are many others. Confucius is simply one example of the non-theistic or atheist philosophers of the East.

There are many more who are less well known in the West. In the West, there is the philosophy of European people before the first life of Jesus Christ. I call it the first life, because officially, he is not dead; he rose after the crucifixion in his spiritual body and has been living as an immortal for the past 2000 or 1968 years as of 2011. Masses of people are confused by this and that's OK.

People think of Jesus Christ as having lived 32 years—the regular mortal style of living up to the crucifixion and after that, he is apparently still alive but everyone is confused about that and what happened afterwards. Whatever one thinks or believes about Jesus Christ, in the Western society philosophy grew before knowledge of this theological philosopher—Jesus Christ spread, and then there is how philosophy was heavily influenced by his teachings and by the organizations that grew up and moved around with his teachings.

There is a good thousand year period of European history when the only philosophy successfully published had been cleared by the Christian clerics, and by people who actually and/or supposedly represented the religious philosophy of Jesus Christ. From the 1750's to 2011, it became increasingly possible in Europe and North America to write and publish works whether they agreed or disagreed with Christian doctrine.

In the pre-Christian realm the philosophies which survived in a way that was actually written down, or that could be written showed up amongst the Greeks and Romans. It is unlikely that these were the only people who practiced some type of philosophical work, but much of the world is oral—sorry, that isn't kinky, it just means spoken and heard rather than written. There are oral traditions today in the world and there always have been. Some are more highly structured than others.

One change which is commonly viewed as a type of cultural progress is the invention and use of the written word. The preservation of knowledge within a culture helps to protect and define it. The preservation of knowledge through a written system means that the information can be added to the gigantic body of knowledge which is sifted by scholars and then taught as curriculum at the world's universities. Once churches and educational systems are using a group of teachings they become quite powerful and can be used across centuries and societies in new ways—in ways that only being able to pass them on through the spoken word could not do.

In Europe one of the places that changed is close to the dawn of this generation's sense of 'history' rather than 'pre-history'. The ancient Greek civilization was not exactly the first, but because they were able to leave traces of teachings and knowledge which have been taught every year to some people ever since, for many they mark the beginning of history. One of their oral tradition philosophers was made immortal by a younger man who had the wealth and the ability to actually write much of it down. This was Socrates and Plato.

Socrates was not a high class man, but was respected as he had fought bravely and loyally for Athens in a number of wars. However, he lived at a time when men in general were expected to do so for their city-state, just as some nations have mandatory military service for men, or even women [as in Israel] in 2011. He made a reputation for himself by trying to find free teachings because he was so poor that he could not afford to buy a local university education. They did have higher education in Athens at the time, but it wasn't for the poor.

Luckily, there were places in Athens where one was allowed to socialize this way. (*The Last Days of Socrates*, Plato, Penguin Classics, Harrold Tarrant 2003). Through such means he met a local nobleman called Plato; this man actually founded or taught at one of the local universities and as part of his service, he wrote numerous dialogues in which this lower class but profound Athenian starred. Thanks to Plato's actions, millions have not only heard of Socrates but have taught at least to some degree his 'elenchus method' of questioning the meanings of words and concepts. This has political implications wherever and whenever one lives and helps to keep philosophy something relevant which people can actually practice today. The other great thing about it, is that once you learn it, it is cheap to do. It can even be free. That doesn't mean one can't spend on it.

Plato taught a number of people, mostly men. One of them was a younger man called Aristotle—who was actually from Macedonia. Aristotle lived during the same time as Alexander the Great. They did not have the Internet and so their view of the world may well have been smaller. Although Alexander the Great was irrelevant in the Americans back then, and in many other locations, he was highly relevant for the Athenians.

Aristotle was able to serve as one of that man's teachers and founded scientific nomenclature by seeing the weird value in simply cataloguing information. Most people who have studied philosophy in West of Kazhakstan on the Earth in 2011 have been introduced to and have heard of Aristotle. These two somehow continue to have an influence in the New Millennium. Christian theology has been affected. One of the main contributions of St. Thomas Aquinas is that he actually sought to bring theology to terms with the heathen pre-Christian thinkers Plato and Aristotle of the Greeks.

Anyone who thinks that was easy is welcome to read The Summa Theologica in an English translation. Originally written in Latin, there is available in the written word in English a brief summary consisting of only 600 pages. There is an outrageously brief book summary of this 'short version' which is only about 20 pages long and is available through BookRags. [Tip: I know because I ghostwrote it, and learned some of these other philosophy bits from doing that]. There are aspects of Jesus Christ's teachings which jibe with a no dualistic view of reality also proposed by Aristotle but these teachings make Jesus Christ's survival of the crucifixion all the more dumfounding but also more consistent.

This book is not really about the history of philosophy as such, but is about how readers can recognize philosophy and how to actually practice it in daily life. The author has received years of training in philosophy and has practiced it both in and out of an academic context for two decades. That's 20 years of practice with academic training to the Master's level. This has included a supplemental year and a half of writing book summaries on philosophical works in 2008 & 2009.

To get back on track: the love of wisdom is what philosophy literally means. Wisdom generally means being able to determine the best course of action in a given situation and taking it. Older people are often associated with wisdom when they are of sound mind because wisdom seems to often improve with life experience. At the same time, at every age, when people look around them some stand out as 'wiser' than the others. There are people who feel this is an innate quality. If so, that does not support philosophy that well as something for the masses. That would make philosophy something for the wise.

Others feel that whatever one's innate ability proper training can make the most of what is there, and that can include wisdom. Say, someone is only average in innate wisdom will be their best with some philosophical training just as the person who works out is going to be in better shape than those who get no exercise regardless of whether or not the person is a natural athlete or naturally strong etc..

This book includes basic mental exercises that everyone can do, that will help them to practice philosophy. The field of philosophy can also be defined as an area that asks a few important, tough questions in life and makes an effort to answer them. Some of the questions are ones also covered by religions and by science, such as: is there a God? And, What is the world really like or made of? This book has a look at these. This book is being written for people who are interested in this subject but may not want to or be able to take university classes or to get degrees in philosophy and theology or religion.

Chapter 2: What is the World Really Like?

The fancy way of saying this is, *What is the nature of reality?*

Well, this is one of those questions that you have to be in the right mood for. There are those to whom seeking an answer is the source of their career. Scientific researchers and clerics are amongst those who, like many of the philosophers, are wondering what the world is really made of—quite literally. Not only that, but 'how do we know what is true and real' and what is illusion?

People who picked up this book who are not interested in this question may just skip it and go to the next chapter. A lot of the people who bought this book, actually like this question, even though it may seem strange if, say, you were just picking out drapes for the living room and suddenly 'there it is, a question about the nature of reality' and do the drapes go to just below the window sill or all the way down to the floor and will they match the sofa? Maybe you really think that way.

OK, well, to start, on a daily basis, it certainly seems as if there is a lot which we take to be the truth. The sky is real, the kitchen is real; the need to buy toilet paper when one runs out is also real. At the same time, there is a lot in the world that doesn't seem to even be real. Silicon breasts are not real in the same sense as natural ones. Lies are real too, but also not the way telling the truth is somehow real in a different way or more real, or real on more levels.

We have our senses and our minds. We have tools of technology and methods for determining what is true and what is false and what is imaginary but shows some type of truth or reality but not on the same level as say, living trees growing in the yard. Fake trees have some kind of reality but we call them fake for a reason. Everyone knows, by the time they are an adult, that there is real grass and there is astro-turf and then there are ideas that some people have about a better type of astro-turf and a superior bred form of organic lawn grass; a kind that doesn't get sick from drought or certain insects for example.

Can our senses and minds be 'trusted' to tell us the truth? This alone has been debated by many of the world's philosophers. The answer seems strange, because it is somehow both yes and no. Yes, it seems that we do reliably learn about the world and how it really works through sensory information. Putting the data from each of the senses together, results in a synthesis which is also reliable. There are also catalogued dysfunctions which can often be treated whether through the use of eyeglasses or 'special training' which permit the dysfunction to be adjusted so that it fits in better with the norm.

Well, that's the short answer regarding the senses, how about the mind part? This is also a matter of some debate. Again, the answer seems to be both yes and no. Throughout the centuries mankind has learned that there are times when we seem to have actually figured out the truth. There are cases where the truth we have determined appears consistent hundreds of years later. Then there are cases where there has been a change, often due to some other discovery. This forces us to adjust our conclusions or to actively participate in deception. For the sake of this discussion let's say that we choose to pursue the truth of a matter.

How do we know what's true? It does still seem that there is a simple enough way of viewing this. Like with most things, those who are interested and go way more deeply into detail and the situation will become more complex. If we take the idea that the information from our senses is accurate and correct, even within a limited way, then we use that. We put that together with our minds. Here, with our minds we tend to add factors such as: if I am getting information from others are they telling me the truth — are they being honest with me? When the answer is 'yes' they are being honest, then there is one other main question: are they correct? When we are reasonably assured that we are being supplied with true, correct information then we use the brain and the sensory information to put together a perception and idea of how something is.

There are cases where what we are taught can be said to help us to see through false appearances. The easiest example of this involves the Sun and the Moon. From the ground, on land, it still seems like they rise, float around in the sky for a while and then sink below the horizon and then repeat the cycle. Most of us, by the time we are full grown have been taught extremely deeply that the Earth is floating through space while spinning and that the Moon is rotating around our planet and traveling together along with other bodies all of which are circling the Sun in the center of our solar system. We are also usually taught about how this wasn't what people had thought before, and then eventually someone figured it out and that it took a very long and a tremendous amount of in-fighting before this new fangled idea was accepted by the Catholics as reflecting the actual truth.

Mathematics and people who have sailed the oceans and those who have used other especial points of observation were involved in figuring this out. That was the Copernican Revolution. Now, we rely on the combination of our mental training and our senses to have our perception that even though it looks like the balls are coming up and going down from many locations on the ground, that isn't exactly what's happening. Still, our language and culture do not seem to have reached a point where instead of saying "the Sun came up" we have changed it to say, "the planet has spun into the Sunlight again"—which is closer to the truth. Dawn occurs when we have rotated into the daylight. This case is not overly complex and is easy enough to understand—it also provides a great example of how language and the mind affect our perception of 'how the world really is'.

Well, that shows how the idea works. So, en masse, humans are aware that there are ways of knowing the truth and ways in which we can be wrong or don't really know. The methods of philosophy—including entelechi and the methods of the social and physical sciences, along with mathematics and logic are all methods which relate to both the mind and the senses and are designed to help humanity to know the truth.

The truth about how the world really is

There are areas where this is easy enough and then there are cases which are rather baffling. There have been philosophers who specialize in the mind and how it relates to 'objects of perception'. In the West, Immanuel Kant, in his classic *The Critique of Pure Reason* provided relatively modern people with one the best and most well organized analysis of the relationship between our senses, our minds and the world itself available. Many readers may well have also heard of Rene Descartes and the popularized version of 'duality'. Duality is the general belief and attitude that the realm of the mind and that of the soul is rather separate from the world of the rest of the senses.

In 2011 neurophysiologists would tend to suggest that the perception of duality is caused itself by the structure of the human brain—the frontal lobes function in a way which can include sensory information and synthesize that but can also operate as if none of the other sensory data were relevant. I suggest, that there is a relationship between the facts and the perception of things but it is also true that in this example we see how challenging it can be to answer these questions about the truth of reality—thoroughly, truthfully and correctly.

Well, most of us go through life with a unique blend of confidence that we have knowledge and experience of the truth—of what the world is really like, how it works in our society and ecological niche, along with mild to extreme uncertainty about the truth. We think, "Well, so I've been told but I don't really know," or "I'm sure that was a lie, but am I right?" and a vast array of other things. "Is there a God?! That's got to be a trick question! How am I supposed to know that?" Meanwhile someone else says, "Of course, there is—only an idiot would think there's no God," and right down the street if you live in an urban place, there is someone who believes that only backward fools indulge in the immature belief in a God the same way that little children play with dolls and recede into realms of fantasy in order to make themselves happy. This is a bit of a problem, simply because in truth: either we cannot tell or a lot of people are wrong. Those who value the truth and think its best when humanity is functioning as close to the truth as possible see that answering this question is actually significant. As I wrote earlier—those not interested may proceed to the next chapter of the book. This is for those who are interested.

In the West, theories and beliefs about how we know anything, including the truth are called epistemology and they are viewed as being their own branch of philosophy. Calling them theories might be misleading, because it shows so much of our own doubts about the conclusions we draw. Scientists and many a philosopher will give the best known explanation for why we think what is true, is true.

The most challenging areas for handling questions about the truth are when we are seeking truth that we don't think can be derived from the senses. In such cases, collecting facts endlessly might be viewed as 'not helping as we had hoped'. There are two ways to go in such cases: 1) although not directly available through the senses, we just need tools to extend the powers associated with the senses to get the truth. Science generally operates from this perspective. Or 2) we have to think about this the right way, and if we do, we will be able to figure out the truth. In a very broad sense, the meditations of the Eastern traditions can be lumped together into this category, but as that is not my specialty, I won't go into it deeply. Mathematics and logic—both ancient and modern, are also methods for 'thinking about things the right way' in order to decipher the truth.

The level of daily life

Dealing with the truth on the level of daily living rather than in a scientific laboratory, is experienced a bit differently. Even so, most thinking people may have noticed that: we have the truths of our senses, the truths of our education, the truths of the day's news, and the cultural context within which we find ourselves. These, along with other ideas floating around in our minds constitute the truth as we find it at 'street level'.

Once we are dealing with cultures then we are also dealing with another level of truth: societal truths. These can even be the so called 'grey areas' between subjective feeling and objective reality.

A general belief or attitude is that in the West at least, when an individual succeeds at being himself or herself there will be a subjective sense of 'what is true' which matches the state of reality outside of the person. This will involve a sense of accuracy about the world as well. The idea that I will function best when I also know what the world is really like, and when I express the way I really am.

Many people who inspect the world around themselves will find that there are truths about which we feel secure, ones that are much more doubtful, there are things we would rather not know, and there is much that we do not know and then there are unknowns from which we protect ourselves. This last part is normally one of ways that people use to protect the personal truth and the private mind from the group situation. This might be defensiveness against family members, a different social group at school, another religion or just an area of personal sensitivity but whatever the reasons; this is one of the things that can be the most exciting for people to work with.

For those who want to actually do philosophy, and not just read about it, finding out how one's private world is and seems and how well or badly it blends with the surrounding, external world is a great project. It can be done inexpensively, and in any neighborhood. You can do it for decades or just once, while waiting for a bus or for a doctor's appointment.

Levels of life

The truth also exists at multiple levels. This doesn't only apply to how it looks through a microscope versus how it looks to the naked eye, but it also means that if you look at societies at the different levels of organization that there are real differences at the different levels. In the human body, this is how there are organs and systems as well as molecules and cells which all come together to form the united whole. The sum of the whole plus the hum of life creates a unity which is radically different from any of the parts taken in and of themselves. Society and its functions can offer real people further opportunities for exploring what is true in the real world. When people live in one place there is a natural tendency to view things through the local truth. It can help to know that the perspective is limited. Still, at least knowing this, one might have a better chance of getting a glimmer of what is beyond, and of truths that transcend.

One of the best reasons for social involvement is to learn about where one is in a system and how one is able to connect with other parts of the same society. The most common key word used for this is 'community.'

The Elenchic Method

One powerful and low cost method for finding more of the truth and more about the truth is called the elenchus. This method was transferred from the oral tradition into the written tradition by Plato, the Athenian from a few centuries before the life of Jesus Christ.

The method is simply to question any given concept. One of the most famous examples that Plato wrote about is 'justice.' What is 'justice?' Through both private thought and group discussion as written in one of Plato's dialogues, the value of this method becomes clear. Many times, we may think we know what we mean with a given word or concept but upon careful examination we find that we didn't. We can also see the weaknesses or flaws in others. When answers to questions are genuinely sought then, this can also yield great rewards. After thorough examination, people end up knowing what they don't know and what they know is often more certain.

Plato was rich and Socrates was poor. The point being, that the elenchus method is free to practice and is useful to people who have money and can be done effectively even if one is poor. It is nice that this is the case, especially in an era where much searching for the truths of life requires expensive scientific equipment and costly years of training in order to practice. That being said, it should be observed that philosophy, as given in this book, is in favor of the use of logic and of the methods of science. Still, for daily living, people need ways of determining the truth.

On the other hand, the Elenchic method requires patience and persistence. To do it, one has to follow a line of questioning and actually answer each question as it comes up before moving on. Logical thinking is supposed to be used to do this. This can be a sticking point since the science of logic was laid out after Plato's life and during the previous 2 thousand years. It has also been developed to quite an extent, an extent which can go beyond what many can deal with. Rather than trying to handle it at a level that goes far beyond one's own capacities, it is best for you to just use the most sensible aspect of your own mind and proceed at your own pace and keep track of what you are doing.

It is okay to take one concept at a time and work through it. This method is obviously for use with concepts and ideas. While it applies well to the abstract realm it is not directly useful but is indirectly very practical. Much like with science, the results are very useful.

Chapter 3: The Question of God—Ontology

Is there a God?

This is the way people living in Christian nations are most likely to see the question. If you don't think you live in a Christian country and need to check, simply ask: do people get Christmas off from school or work because that is a major holiday? If the answer is yes, then you live in a Christian community. If this is true throughout the nation in which you live, then you are living in a Christian country. If the answer is no, then the opposite is true. The main holidays in your country reflects your 'state religion'.

This book has the limited bias of an author who has only lived in Christian nations unlike such people 500 years ago. However, the author has been repeatedly presented with various religious and philosophical viewpoints including atheism in multiple forms and much of it as part of the philosophical training which helped qualify the author to write you this book. In this, the term Christian does not mean "right wing conservative sect led by televangelists"—it just means: most of the churches are Christian, pretty much everyone has heard of Jesus Christ and the majority of the nation's citizens have already been 'saved' at some point during their lives even if they resent the idea that their souls had needed saving before they were saved.

A childish but powerful way of emphasizing what I mean is how many of the Christians I'm talking about grumble at least once in a while about Christianity but the minute anyone threatens to not give presents at Christmas or chocolate bunnies at Easter they are all about keeping the Christianity—at least in that sense.

Well, okay then, one of the main parts of Christianity is that there is God. What are the basic supports of this? This is a philosophy book and we are seeking the truth in a world which is not always, but sometimes puzzling. There are those who view the entire manifest cosmos as evidence in favor of God's existence. Some claim that whatever God is; caused the Big Bang and the rest is continuing after effects of that.

The official Catholic view, shared by many sects of Protestants is that God has crafted the physical universe, has envoys to help and protect humanity but otherwise remains aloof from the activities on Earth. There are scholars of history—especially those in India, who used the word Indra and called "a god"—what Christian readers would probably have interpreted as "God" to cover the basics about the manifest universe. If someone asked, "Mommy, why is the sky the sky?" Mommy might make her own life easier by saying, "Indra." That seems to be the level at which Indra meant god.

Throughout history, the Western philosophers would often interpret the natural order of the world, including mathematics, as evidence in favor of the existence of God. Other philosophers and their students have argued about this because there were a few hundred years there where all the people in Christian countries had to support God if they wanted to be published and not arrested by local police or stoned, or otherwise punished. In reality, there were mathematicians who were sincere in their belief in God, and others who didn't really believe it but felt coerced by the culture of the day. Remember, figuring out what your culture is doing to you, as you quest for the truth is part of what you're dealing with.

In 2011 Plato and Aristotle are still taught because their work was incredibly powerful. So much so, in fact, that over 1200 years after their lives ended, Thomas Aquinas valiantly helped the Catholic church face the ideas of Plato and Aristotle head on without being dismissive. The fast answer is that those ancient Greeks believed in what are commonly referred to in Jewish and Christian circles as "false gods". This might well have been the top of the social hierarchy, when the Kings or Pharoah and entourage were considered to actually be gods. The Jews and Jesus Christ explained that no, their God created the manifest world and was not simply the son of the previous king.

For those who do believe in God, the puzzling thing about using the created world as evidence on God's behalf is the church doctrine that God is not really in the world although He made it.

What else is used in the main arguments supporting the existence of God? The primary ones are 'scriptures'—holy written works which have been attributed to God. The main thing with these is that people understand two main qualities: 1) they are works of nonfiction. 2) they include some references and metaphors and world views which are so steeped in a very different cultural and historical context that many readers in 2011 would find they do not make sense or the meaning cannot be properly determined. Even so, they provide a specific effort to document some of the messages and movements of God in relation to some groups of people on the face of the Earth and as such provide evidence in the same sense that witnesses are considered valuable in court cases. Numerous eye witness and audio accounts of God are described throughout The Bible. However, the appearances are rare compared to say, rainy weather, but possibly as frequent as "a solar eclipse".

There is another important factor regarding the question of the existence of God. There is a special term for it in philosophy called "Ontology". This is about the very basis of being. Now, here we have a few schools of thought. Again, this is relying on the Western philosophical tradition. West meets East now and then, which is excellent and necessary, and some of same conclusions are re-confirmed whereas other views reach a higher stage of development. Since the author is far more educated in Western philosophy it makes sense that most explanations will have this bias and benefit.

Ontology is about the very basis of everything. For some, this is not considered important. However, in relation to the question of God's existence it can be very important.

The issue now comes to interpreting Nature itself. Thanks to scientific research most of us have heard of the molecular, atomic and even subatomic realms. Also, most have been taught that light can manifest in wave form and particular form. Finally, the majority of readers in 2011 have some awareness that sound waves and other invisible but perceptible waves do affect us. What does this have to do with God? Well, is the true nature of matter actually spirit and the spiritual? Some Eastern and Western philosophers might see this as a matter of semantics, or a rehash of whether or not the thing exists outside of the mind or if the 'group mind' of humanity is only able to perceive a certain way.

Are the ultimate building blocks of matter spiritual in essence and in form? This is a fundamental question. For many, the significance is great. If the manifest world, Nature and humankind are built out of spirit, then for many, this is a persuasive argument in favor of the existence of God.

If the ultimate building blocks of matter are not linked to God, then we are pushed back to seeing the entire natural world as perhaps, made by Indra...or as not so able to be used as evidence for the reality of God's existence.

There are schools of philosophical thought in which the spiritual does not automatically mean support of the argument in favor of God's existence. However, in any Christian nation or in any worldview which is deity oriented, especially the monotheistic religions it is the dominant interpretation: when matter comes from Spirit we see it is God's handiwork as readily as a parent recognizes his or her own offspring.

For people who do not conclude the existence of a God from the manifest universe, then this part of the argument is not as relevant to answering the question about God.

It is for these reasons, that ontology—the matter of what is the actual basis of the world is so relevant to arguments about God's existence.

What does ontology have to do with the human mind? Well, there are schools of thought that view the mind—the human capacity to think as well as to feel and to do, as being 'the spirit of mankind'. Others would cite the life force—which is both obvious yet ephemeral.

There are those who claim that any gods, even Jesus Christ, are essentially the invention of the human mind or society. There are those who claim that the essence of monotheism is that God is absolute and objective in nature and not dependent upon humans any more than the next star over, let alone the one lighting up our planet, are dependent upon our thinking in order to be real. The author admits that in the course of this, there are times when what I write will include 'extensions' off the original meaning.

For instance, having been born in 1968 rather than 1025, I naturally think of the entire solar system and galaxies when I think of the manifest Cosmos whereas in 1025 I might have thought out as far the stars I could see at night in the sky but beyond that I would have not had any information. The whole Christian idea of God's purpose for humanity, and the true cause of the benevolence is simply that since humans are sentient, we can actually be aware of God and self-aware at the same time. This enhances the experience for God rather than only having stones around. While comical in the extreme: thinking human here—rock on the ground there, this is pretty much the normal Christian viewpoint. Which does more for me as a conscious being? Only on a bad day is the rock going to win...

The Eastern philosophers have a very important, sometimes complicated 'thing' about how subject and object are related and how these co-create everything from identity to fried fish. For those who want to explore more in another direction after this book: that attitude recombines what in the West are called ontology or metaphysics with epistemology—knowledge and the mind. People like that are more likely to perceive how a God or gods can be both real and the creation of humankind, rather than seeing them as 'false gods' because their existence relies on being perceived by humans.

For the sake of this book, the author believes that there is a benevolent and objectively real God, the Son of whom told all the humans to rely on Him in all efforts to relate to his Father for reasons unknown or easily misunderstood. The author was raised Unitarian Universalist, which is loaded with nominal Christians, humanists and outright atheists and well read people with their own take on things. The views in this book reflect the thinking of the author and are not representative of every Unitarian Universalist (UU). In fact, if you want to start an argument in a UU congregation just bring the book and treat the people drinking coffee after the service as if they agree with what this book says and tell them about it and within half an hour you should have found supporters, opponents and the indifferent.

Besides, the author believes that Jesus Christ actually was a Messiah and a demi-god, type of God and is both impressed by the miracles and acknowledges that these were events which are actually harder to believe than most lies we hear in our daily lives. The fact that miracles are scientific anomalies makes a wonderful side discussion for those interested.

Those deeply into side issues, may also want to follow through by learning all about how some of the Eastern philosophers, adepts and yogis seem to achieve results with proper mind training which defy normal Western society standards.

Now and then, a Westerner goes on a retreat and walks on coals without getting burned and that's great for the person but adds to the claims of both our Jesus Christ of the West and the adepts of the

East who have been telling us that these kinds of results are possible since before Jesus was born.

The remaining evidence of God's existence are more dubious because they do not stand up to the same type of scientific scrutiny. The best way that some of the other evidence can be evaluated using Western methods is to use techniques of the social scientists.

There are definite challenges involved in rating the subjective experiences of individuals and using that as further 'testimony' in favor of God's existence. Nevertheless, this and a few other phenomenon such as healing by laying on of hands and the like are often treated as evidence by some and scoffed at by others as impossible rubbish.

What about me?

OK, this book is intended to empower readers to actually practice philosophy for themselves. So, how does this help you? You need to figure out where you stand about the 'basis of the universe' issue. You need to know whether or not you are in a situation where you have to assume or presume God's existence or not. If you do, then the rest of your philosophizing is coming from this basis. That's ok, but it is helpful for you to be self - aware of that. If not, then this is also useful, because it affects how you will tend to interpret certain events and phenomenon in life.

On the other hand, if you do not believe in God, or are definitely not sure—many people truly believe that we have no way of knowing whether or not there is a God, then when it comes time to do work on ethics and morality it will be relevant.

It will also strongly influence the way you approach religion, other philosophy and the whole issue of 'the spiritual'. If it doesn't seem like it matters, see if you can figure out why you think it doesn't.

To make the best progress it will help if you become clear on what you personally think counts as reliable information: is it science, a religious viewpoint, certain scriptures, your mother, the clerics, the news, your senses? Once you know, make an effort to stick to conclusions based upon only those types of information. Doing that means you are practicing philosophy. In so doing, you will not be a drone or a brainwashed monkey, but a functioning person able to think for yourself.

The author does not presume everyone will always agree but does believe that in at least some of this, there is a right answer and a wrong one, just as we get with math and whether or not the brighter of the 2 big lights in the sky is a star at the center of our solar system and not your imagination in a universe in which only you exist. Even so, it is the reader's own responsibility to agree or disagree.

What are gods? Are there a bunch of them rather than just one?

The simple, popular description of gods is; entities which have supernatural abilities. They may or may not have human forms. They may or may not have forms which humans can recognize in nature.

In some societies the upper class was called gods. It is my personal belief that ancient Egypt's under Pharoahs and the Greek Olympians and probably also the Asatru "Odin and Frigg, etc" were all of this kind. Even today, the Emperor of Japan is held to be a living god by those keeping the old tradition. The Tibetan Buddhists are similar, where their kings and chief clerics are the same people. It may be worth noting that this is what Pontious

Pilate thought Jesus Christ was: that's why he called him The King of the Jews—their king and their spiritual leader. Depending on the religion of the place, the leaders and their people may well have believed this was the truth. Others may have thought it was a propaganda program which most people never fell for but no one would tell the leaders that when they didn't want to get killed. This is a reminder that silence is as likely to mean disagreement as agreement, but for some reason it often feels as if others agree when they keep silent.

This seems like an ancient idea but in reality, in 2011, the Emperor and possibly also the Empress of Japan are actually gods according to the local religion and customs. In reality "its not just them." There are a number of societies in the 21st century that have multiple human incarnate gods. These are not the type of god that has the power to have created the entire cosmos and in that respect, by comparison they are very much 'small gods'.

In the USA and many other Western nations there are multiple perceptions of gods. Most commonly, the people are monotheistic or agnostic or atheistic about 'the One true God' which has the power to do everything from cause the entire universe to manifest and yet is so thorough as to care about both you and your little sister and the insects in your back garden.

Then there are the 'small gods' of popular culture. Usually, when people call a human a god—it is mainly a special compliment. In a way, no one takes such remarks seriously, but the only reason anyone uses this phrase as a compliment is to acknowledge that the human exhibit's a power which comes across as supernatural or overwhelming and incredible. Examples include people like the drummer Neil Peart, who has been called by many a god of rock-n-roll drumming. Naturally, culturally, no one takes this seriously except that people do. How good is his drumming? So good, that people have called him a god, rather than a regular human being. This isn't entirely useless, but the divine powers are limited. Don't expect him to be able to take care of all problems just because he has the drumming power.

Small gods throughout history have often been 'more like that'. They are much more like normal humans in that even their divine powers are not all encompassing. Since they often were members of the upper classes or had other human forms, they had limitations even though they were divine. Most Americans and other Westerners came across these in history lessons. The gods of the Greeks and Romans seemed to be like that: small gods, who had personalities and everything else. In the Far East, they have a very complicated situation with small gods, both in India and in East Asia.

It's complicated because they have a very long history with gods. There are multiple reasons why people are called gods over there. The peoples deal with gods in more than one way. The people relate their gods to the local religions in more than one way. Also, in reality, being an American trained in Western traditions, I only have a little information about it all, and none of it is in cultural context.

Same issue, different angle

In the Western nations, especially the Far West—Western Europe and the Americas, there were small gods prior to the arrival of Christianity. The dominant religions which held these for 1000 years or more are still around: Druidry in Britain and the West of Europe and also what is called Asatru—the old religion of much of Scandinavia.

Since Christianization, most of those deities are not taken seriously; they are not viewed by most people as 'real gods'. The nicest thing anyone can say of them is that they are or were 'small gods' or were demoted from having been gods. Nevertheless, they still have their fans. Ceridwen is a goddess of Druidry, Freya the Asatru goddess had a consort, Odin who is somehow still famous as well as his son Thor. Thor's sister Freya was actually a goddess of love. Their stories go on and on. Somehow, they exist in the 21st century as part of an underground movement or in the form of popular culture.

In 2011 there was a movie about the Asatru: the god Thor has continued to be extremely popular in Northern North America thanks to a comic book and has even had a film deal. The common image or attitude seems to be that Thor doesn't even mind that much if the common people don't believe he is a real deity as long as they've heard of him and think he's really awesome.

Naturally, people in general are still impressed by the power of thunder and lightning. The old story is that thunder is the sound of the god Thor fighting with giants using his hammer Mjolnor. This still impresses people and it has contributed to the continuance of Thor's reputation amongst humanity.

What made the gods—gods in Druidry and Asatru? In truth, people are not certain. It is debatable. Most of the records are gone, as they were oral—spoken and heard, rather than written words and lessons. There are people in the 21st century who practice these religions, but even those who do may not relate to 'the gods and goddesses' the same way as people did centuries ago. That being said, it might be a mistake to assume that people were stupid just because they lived a long time ago. After all, the words and knowledge of some very brilliant people have found their way to 2011 and continue to impress people.

Goddesses

In reality, in North America and the Far West of Europe, the known religions which developed there before Christianity was imported from the Mediterranean and Arabia/Persia/Middle East there were goddesses and gods. This is known as polytheism. A lot of women and men prefer that the deities were as likely to be feminine as masculine. On a purely political level, a lot of women and many of the men, prefer including goddesses feeling that it is more fair and closer to the truth.

One aspect of this involves how people relate to the divine. People find it easier to emulate beings of the same biological sex than to members of the opposite sex—at least some of the time, but people also naturally feel intense desires to feel a strong connection to members of the opposite sex as well. When there are both gods and goddesses, people find this resolves some issues of relating.

The main problem is how the Christian world copes with these same issues in a world where there is only one deity: God, and that deity is male or is of a nature which would be most accurately interpreted by humans on Earth as male. There are still female images and conceptions of the divine, but they are not treated quite the same way; not necessarily seen as literally deities—but still indicative of truths.

Mother Nature and the Mother of All Creation are phrases used in the late 20th and 21st centuries [Christian calendar / 48th century in the Hebrew and Chinese calendars] which point to reality in a way often associated with the divine. This entity, or one like it—perhaps a sister, has also been written of in The Bible as "the Queen of Heaven". Christianity has included these truths through the virgin Mother of God and a variety of Saints.

Regarding this matter, the Christian denominations have a strange situation. The Catholics have had more female saints and have harbored nuns for over a thousand years, but do not allow women priestesses. The Protestants have neglected female saints for centuries but have adopted women priestesses before the Catholics have. There is a great deal of ignorance and confusion regarding how to interpret the role of Nuns within, but especially outside of the Catholic type of Christianity. They are some type of cleric but are not priestesses. There is a lot of mutual and one sided forms of ignorance about this.

In general, the denominations that have started allowing women clergy—priestesses, do not have a history of having monastic orders for males or for females. In those denominations, the efforts of people would have played out more through the roles that lay people can have in a church. In congregational life, especially in communities that rely heavily on their churches, there are numerous roles for the lay people to fulfill. People who are not experienced or deeply involved with their religions may not be very aware of these things. That contributes to the confusion and in many cases, also to the frustration. In some respects it comes back to issues surrounding, money and power and fame. Most religious feats and deeds are done by people who are not famous. This is true in every walk of life, not only in religion. Still, as people grow up and learn about life, we discover the famous people and may draw some correct and incorrect conclusions about life from this. So, invisibility is a characteristic of many, especially in relation to the media and mass publicity.

Goddesses have been and are still found in 'small god' religions, such as Wicca, Asatru and Druidry in the Far West and North America. Culturally, these peoples, even those who are truly and devoutly Christian will readily admit the truth of the dictum, "In the eyes of the child, God is the Mother," and therefore, a goddess form.

In popular culture, the goddesses outside of the family life are usually either artists—such as musicians, or extremely sexually attractive to men or both. So, goddesses of sexual love and goddesses of music are the most commonly adored and recognized. They are liable to be called 'stars' rather than goddesses but the main idea is the same.

There are goddesses more devoted to women or who are more refined in certain of their attributions; these are most likely to be making headway for humanity by making progress for women en masse. Remember, the whole truth about women's liberation is that it releases men from a variety of evils as part of the same process. Politicians, midwives and women advocating for other women and still protecting children, especially the ones that are able to do so without being the absolute enemy of "the men" or "the wrong kind of women" are the most profound. Most of these are invisible, but now and then one gets noticed. In this regard public figures who are successful women may not be treated by the culture as actual goddesses outright, but may be seen as more intimately connected with 'the Goddess' than many.

In the monotheistic reality, all the small gods get re-categorized. They are either 'small gods,' 'false gods,' 'saints but not gods' or 'folk heroes but not deities'. Their best chance would be to be seen as 'an emanation' which is another way of saying the same thing, the beam of sunshine is not the Sun itself except that they obviously have the same essence or it wouldn't be called sunshine.

It is true that there has been some exchange of ideas between the Western and Eastern cultures for thousands of years. Some of life in these places is the same and some of it is different. As always, I acknowledge my own limitations. The whole thing is coming from a legitimate and limited cultural and historical context. In actual fact, one of the greatest developmental leaps of the cultures of the Far West in the late 20th century has been to see how, even after the tremendous effort of at least 2 centuries to establish truly objective knowledge and methods that secure it: there are times and ways in which it is impossible to surmount the limitations of 'perspective'. This has actually been a hard lesson for those dedicated, especially through the sciences and philosophy, let alone religion, to find objective reality while being a human being. The European Enlightenment became engrossed with this, and much of the work of philosophers such as

Immanuel Kant, as well as people such as Rene DesCartes, Leibniz and more contemporary thinkers really was all about determining which aspects of reality are the human mind or society, and what is actually the truth and how to find and share knowledge of objective reality from within the human existence.

Objective reality, and the Absolute, means: the truth of things that have no dependence upon human perception for their reality or existence. This is something which is very tied up with the question of God in Western humanity. One of the fundamental qualities of the One God is that this God has no dependence upon humanity or human perception to exist. The dependence is entirely one sided, it is not 'interdependent' at all: humans cannot exist without God and God can easily exist without humans. That's really how it works.

In this tradition, the best humans can do is to unite with this God and the highest accomplishment of humanity in relation to this God other than love is the story that God made humanity in order to develop 'self awareness'. So, the sentience of humanity, could almost be construed as a vanity of God, to have a type of being that can actually recognize the being and nature and reality of God rather than blundering along caught up in it, but oblivious to it. This is the God that makes 'small gods' of all the others.

What are gods? Are there a bunch of them or just one or none?

This is the same question that was asked at the beginning of this chapter. So far, the theory that there is no God, nor gods, has not been addressed. Here it is: given that the author admits to not agreeing with this theory, here it is.

There have been atheists throughout millenia, just as there have been devotees of one or more God or gods throughout the ages. It is also not a new idea or belief in itself. It shows up in more than one region of the Earth just as spontaneously as do theories involving gods or a God. One of the most famous atheists in the Western tradition of philosophy is David Hume. He wrote in Britain in the 1700s. He was followed by people such as Friedrich Nietzsche in the 1800s and people like Bertrand Russell in the 1800s & 1900s.

All of the forces of Nature, which have conspired to create the manifest world and known universe are not somehow "divine" and calling them "God" is a real mistake. The order of the universe may be amazing but does not indicate any innate intelligence and there are no emotional implications of it whatsoever. In Western philosophy, there was one theory that described the God as being 'the watch maker who has nothing to do with the watch once it has been made', only this theory that there may be the Big Bang but there is nothing divine or sentient about it, takes the whole thing a step further.

Another necessary belief or conclusion for full fledged and pervasive atheism, would be to discard all the historical notions and examples of deity as in fact having been 'false gods', but for an entirely different reason than the theist or monotheist dismisses them. They are the invention of human kind. Instead of making the claim that this makes them, or the upper class—sometimes called the upper 'crust' deities, it just shows how much this is just something people made up.

The gods were a simplistic effort of people in power to describe to the common people abstractions such as law and order and power. They anthropomorphized and made up stories. This was a great way for teaching people at a certain level but for those who were able to attain beyond that level, these kinds of beliefs fell away like outmoded leaves from a tree that has blossoms.

So, there may be advancements in consciousness and understanding and knowledge and experience that cause people to outgrow the gods. For those who reach that level, then the world is the same but different than it was before.

What then of super powers or even just strange and amazing abilities? Well, the atheist would say that either they are illusions—intentionally or accidentally created. If not that, then they are just natural talents or events: instead of supernatural, it was natural. Its that simple.

Where does this leave ethics and morality? In the hands of mankind alone. Many fear this and others really don't. Right and wrong; good and bad will be pursued further in the next chapter.

Chapter 4: Good & Evil / Right & Wrong

Good & Evil

Due to the nature of this topic, it will be covered in terms of 'lines of thinking' more than once, to see it from different angles and so readers can see how the arguments take shape.

Discussion 1: Right & Wrong

Well, this is obvious, except when it isn't. Most people are dimly aware of having instincts about morality and receiving education about it. Early childhood includes a lot of this type of education. Those who become parents review the entire process of how basic ethics are taught and are reminded of what people are like before they know.

Good and evil can be seen as relating to the types of emotions involved with experiences or can be viewed in terms of the results of actions or by looking at the processes involved. There are also causes and results. Most people have heard of intentions: these can be specific purposes, such as building a house or a school, achieving enlightenment or making a painting. Good intentions are those meant to benefit anyone affected as well as the person who takes action with intentions.

But, what is it?

[Someone raises the hand, like when we were children in school—the teacher instructed the students to raise a hand signaling the need to ask a question or make a comment without interrupting the teacher-this is wise.] "But what *are* good and evil?"

Your right, let's back up and start there. Let's start with Good. What is it? First qualities that come to mind are: pleasure, love, kindness, helping others, happiness. Second qualities that come to mind are more about seeing the world as including both self and other: to do good is often to refrain from trampling over the wills of other people. Third: that brought up controlling ourselves and others. As far as we can tell this is not always wrong nor is it always correct. It can be challenging to handle this the best way.

OK, so in general, anything one does that brings pleasure to oneself or to others without harming others is good. In general, helping other people without harming their person's or their wills is also good. This is how simple yet powerful 'the Good' is.

Readers are aware that for some reason, these simple truths become distorted or twisted from being obviously good into something bad. That will be covered more later.

What about the world?

The discussion of 'the Good' above, was centered around humans. Well, what about the rest of the world, with all the animals and plants? What about the rest of the universe for that matter? Can the Good be extended to include immeasurable distances?

The simple answer is 'yes', the same principle that makes an action or idea or attitude 'Good' for humans can also be applied to other creatures and to the world in general. When we consider 'the world as a whole' then we learn to see it a bit differently. The entire matter of environmentalism is rooted in this realization that the world is a unity even with all of the diversity. The whole thing is interdependent and all those items in the shops that seem at the consumer end as if they came from nowhere, have all come from somewhere. Most of us know this, but the awareness tends to be very dim, perhaps especially for people in the West due to the specialization of labor and delivery. The majority of environmentalism comes back to the basic principles above. What gives pleasure, what might cause harm? How much can be taken and how from anywhere without wreaking havoc elsewhere?

It is actually in seeking to answer this question, that humanity in general is forced back into the simple questions of how to receive good without causing harm to others. Let's face it, most of those who have cable television enjoy it, but these same people were not necessarily in favor of making tens of thousands of other people starve or end up impoverished and imprisoned because of 'the redistribution of resources'. Again: so much is hidden between one end of the experience and the other, but most of the time, that is where our real ethical problems lie.

Real conflict can emerge when there is not enough for two, but there are two. Both have the equal right to life and happiness. Now, is it possible to find an actual 'Good' solution to such a situation or do the circumstances themselves force competitive conflict? This is important, but due to the focus of this chapter, this will stop right here. So, the main conclusion is that implementing 'the Good' becomes much more complicated once humans are dealing with the full scale of life throughout the planet and across species in addition to dealing with it within a family or between two individual humans. This is still using the very clear, simple principles found at the beginning of the discussion.

Most of the American readers have heard the saying, "The road to Hell is paved with good intentions." Essentially, this is the warning that 'good intentions alone are not really enough' and that sometimes efforts to do good go awry, often due to lack of information.

What is evil?

This is also sometimes obvious, but not always. Malice is generally considered to be evil. The emotions of hatred and rage and deep sorrow, jealousy and revenge are most commonly associated with evil. Selfishness when done incorrectly, is normally considered to be evil.

When people take good care of themselves and pursue their own interests while still being considerate of others and with compassion and care then this is healthy self-interest although it can also be described as selfishness by others who don't like it. For a long, deep and complex discussion of selfishness please Ayn Rand's Objectivist philosophy as she covered this very well. Also, people who have been oppressed during cultural history may be in the process of learning to assert their own needs and rights. This means that for them, it is healthier to behave 'more selfishly'. Others, who have the opposite problem, need to learn to be less selfish.

In the second set of qualities about 'the Good' it was observed that restraint and consideration of the wills of others is highly important. In reality, the types of evil associated with selfishness are typically failures to use that power of self-restraint, or adjustment of one's own behavior, out of consideration of others. In this respect, the similarity of Good and Evil can be frightening. The exact same behavior, as an individual or group can instantly turn from Good to Evil or the other way around based upon its effect on others. If the others like it and also benefit, and no harm is done, then it's actually Good. If the others don't will it, want it or like it, the deed is now Evil.

Often, people are not confused about this, but when viewed closely, it becomes clear: 1) why this can be confusing at times, and 2) there is an important side issue about control.

Control is important in relation to oneself and others and the world. Children often need the benefit of their parents' and elders control. Yet, children are also vulnerable to the misuse of control by their elders. For adults, employers or the demands of a business operation, lovers, other adults, and children are the main other people with whom there are apt to be issues about control.

Culture, and religion and governments as well as businesses and schools and families all influence people. Within these social environments people either exert control or do not. Leadership is when one person exerts control or influence over others. Then, obviously, the more leadership duties an individual has, the more important it is to be able to control others so that the actions are Good rather than evil. Most adults experience this in their personal and working lives. One of the worst things about a 'bad job match' is that the effect is often evil because of the sensitive relationship between Good action and Bad action. Bad leadership, evil control of others is one of the worst events that can occur in the world.

What else?

The worst of evils is generally considered to be the actual enjoyment of bringing harm to others either directly or indirectly. This makes sense when there is no question that survival for all involved, and decent quality of life would occur if no harm were done.

It is because of this that conflict and issues surrounding resources is of such prominence in the world. Essentially, when evil occurs because it has been somehow forced by other factors, it is still a problem but is not exactly the same as when someone sets out to do evil for its own sake and 'as evil per se'.

Here is an example of evil occurring from good intentions of one person, and 3rd party ignorance. A child wants a video game. A parent wants to make the child happy. One parent goes to the other. The other parent goes out and extorts someone else to get the money for the video game. The child soon receives the video game. The extorting parent has obviously done evil. Both the child and the other parent have contributed greatly to the other one committing the evil act. The child, being a minor, would generally be viewed as 'blameless', even though the good intention of making the child happy was there. The person who did the extorting did the worse evil by committing the illegal crime to get the money, and then turned around and did the good act of getting the child a desired toy out of real love and a sense of parental responsibility. This is one way in which "the world goes crazy". People who feel it is easy enough to work respectably and to get plenty of funding for video games without harming others might see this as ridiculous. However, severely poor people full of desires for a better life and desperate, might find the message hits 'too close to home'.

So, then, there is evil which is done 'as evil' with the person who does it self-aware that the course of action is wrong doing. This might well not be the majority of evil which occurs in the world. Much of it, so much of it; takes place despite at least some good intentions. Life's situations are sometimes complex enough that reaching clarity on whether some course of action is Good or Bad can be challenging, even though the underlying principles are simple.

Conclusions?

To reiterate, here are the basic qualities of evil: malicious intentions. Actions which will not benefit those affected, or who will suffer worse harm than they do benefit from the activities. The second set of qualities is simple indifference to the welfare of others, including those most directly affected by one's actions. The basic qualities of good are: bringing of benefit to others- this is also true when the doer benefits from the activity, and causing pleasure. The second type of quality is the consideration of others; this often results in refraining from taking actions or in altering how one does one's own will in any given situation.

In truth, this is the main reason why military personnel and other warriors are often in a difficult situation. It seems they either choose to, or are often forced to 'do evil in the service of the good'—or what is ardently hoped to be the service of the good.

This is also one of the main criticisms made by civilians in nations that have voluntary-only military service: pacifists blame the soldiers for having made the evil decision to be soldiers in the first place—because of the kinds of situations they are more likely to be in by being soldiers.

For nations that have military veterans, this can be part of the overall dilemma for civilians and soldiers in the same society.

What about me?

This book is intended to be practical. So, how can readers use the above in order to actively practice philosophy? Evaluate your own perceptions of Good & Evil in relation to the above. If it fits, use this approach when considering taking action in life. If it doesn't, see what doesn't work. If nothing else, become clear on how you actually make your judgments about good and evil in your daily life.

Discussion 2 Good & Evil as Right & Wrong

In simple terms, ethics are what morality is without religion. A funny but rather true way of saying it would be to observe that ethics is what your parents teach you, morality comes from the church minister. Obviously, it's either pretty much the same thing, or else its exactly the same thing.

Right and wrong is easily understood in terms of early childhood development. For everyone who is not a parent or has not spent a lot of time watching parents of young children in action, this is probably nothing more than vague subconscious memories.

When care givers are patient and loving in disposition, yet attentive a lot of the care is to provide correction and direction to growing entities. Here, from the perspective of an innocent child and when seen with the eyes of love of care givers who view the baby or toddler as good: there is a perception of natural order and a sense of chaos. This chaos is not big nasty and evil. This chaos is immature, and doesn't know any better and so has to be protectively taught everything from 'don't bite the other children', 'share toys', and don't drink laundry detergent. This is learning right from wrong. Then people grow up and begin to attend school or receive home schooling and tutoring. Right and wrong become a little more complicated simply because more is involved than there was before.

This process continues, only more people contribute to what they view as right and wrong. Naturally people notice that there are trends—people agree and disagree with one another. There is a lot of common ground, which helps the general order in most societies. Some of the rules people tend to take 'for granted' throughout many societies.

One major way that people observe cultural differences in when they run into abnormal regulations—things that just are considered acceptable in their own culture but are suddenly rejected in another or the other way around—where what they view as criminal at best is treated as acceptable by the general populace.

Religion has usually become apparent by the age of 10 years if not earlier and some semblance of order is developed. Religion reinforces a lot of what is already known to be right or wrong. There are also instructions, or advice which is more specific to a given denomination or whole religion. There are times when these clash with each other. In the most extreme cases—we have the history of religious wars. Religious traditions have their own internal recommendations about these things. In these cases, people are more liable to think in terms of morality than ethics.

Adolescence, the onset of parenting, the midlife crisis, the onset of old age are all times in life where questions concerning ethics and morality surge. One reason has to do with self-identity and with one's sense of place in society. This includes peer relationships and subcultures. Subcultures abound in North America, whether based around the church one goes to, or the drugs one uses, or the music listened to, or the fashion or the amount of money, whether the parents are married to one another or not and so on it goes. There are so many ways in which people choose this way or that as being their right or wrong.

During youth, school, family and friends are the main thing, but as adults work and family—with friends following are the areas of life where ethical decision making are the most frequent. Community and society follow on, being linked of course to the politics of the state and that of the religion. People make decisions about this daily. Fortunately much of it is easy; we develop reasonably good habits of doing right—at least as far as we know. Somehow life has a way of throwing challenges into people's lives. Somewhere, many adults are facing an ethical quandary.

So, people learn to a limited degree which sets of ethics and morality go with which religion and subculture within their own nation. People learn about whom they are and who their parents or friends want them to be. There is a dichotomy involved for many people in which there is a sense that "No matter what one does, there will always be someone out there who feels it's wrong." Condemnation seems universally available. Luckily, approval is also often something people can find. It is common practice for there to be groups labeled as evil—often they are composed of people who actually are, and this is only intentional sometimes. In some cases, they have been forced into such roles by other elements of society. The main crimes in society are the ones agreed upon to be Evil or "most wrong."

Now, one of the questions asked is: are they wrong only because the society says so? Some regulations, those which most help or harm the lives of human beings are considered the most serious. While there are people who insist that yes, even laws against rape and murder are "socially constructed ethics" many other people disagree. Religion and masses of people feel that such societal rules are deeper than 'social conformity'. Religions, especially the dominant monotheistic worldviews: Christianity, Islam and Judaism all agree. Major other religions in the world normally agree. Such things are either basic to human nature—the sense of basic human kindness and mutual respect. Others view these as taught, but primitive "Don't bite the other children, and when you are an adult don't rape or kill anyone, and don't drink Drano." In reality, the argument against drinking Drano is most likely to be viewed as "socially constructed" because Drano is manmade. Don't drink poison, is simply viewed as "sound advice for the masses".

In truth, people continue to debate the following: Are morality and ethics something exist in 'the Absolute'—this is objective truth. For those who believe in God, these are the rules as God has made them in his loving perfect wisdom. For those who do not believe in God, this argument tends to be weaker but still finds support amongst those who believe in absolute truths, and objective reality. The ultimate ground of morality as 'absolute' can function whether people believe in the truth as being able to exist entirely externally and independently of mortals, or whether that 'Absolute' is in the mind as a spiritual truth which can filter down into ordinary consciousness. In either case, religion and sometimes philosophy and transcendental practices assure people that humans can really know this. Once it is knowledge, then it falls away as belief.

This creates a changed social dynamic because, even when one is convinced that one bears knowledge 'true justified belief' one can easily come across others who will fiercely oppose and insist that you back off enough to call your knowledge belief. Those who refuse find that there are some other members of the same civilization with whom it is not possible to get along in certain ways. Such people can usually survive working at the same workplace or attending the same school but the more they wear their deep seated differences of knowledge and belief on their sleeves the harder it is to deny the conflict.

In order to even survive this, people who function in a society where tolerance is expected, will find that they need to believe that it is okay to call their knowledge beliefs, at least some of the time. This doesn't mean that anyone has to like it.

Now where are we?

One bottom line here is that even when one is very clear about oneself it will be situation where there is a lot of common ground with millions, maybe even billions of people and other creatures worldwide. Even so, there are going to be groups of people who disagree, some weakly or meekly and others aggressively. This is probably true for everyone alive.

There either actually is Right and Good in ways that go beyond 'socially constructed rules' that people simply invent or else there aren't. It can be helpful for people to be aware of what they are resting their general beliefs and attitudes on. In fact, I have met people who believe in the Absolute Truth. I have met people who honestly feel they only behave well thanks to fear of God which is similar to fear of one's parents during childhood only better. I have met people who claimed to argue for nonduality. I have met people who do not believe in any deity who think that social rules are good enough and that looking more deeply into this issue doesn't even help. Well, the author believes that one of the best teachings of the ancient Athenian Socrates was that he did this kind of thing amongst his friends: simply actually look into what we claim we think or know. Either we come up with greater clarity and get rid of a lot of ignorance we had floating around or else we discover that we didn't even actually know what we were talking about, and have a lot to learn. When one discovers a gap, and is aware of it, then people can be more open to learning. When one finds out for certain the why and the what of one's beliefs—and knowledge, then a personal sense of security about it sets in in a wonderful way.

What's that?

This poking around into things, using key words or rooting around to find out what one thinks by asking and answering questions is what was called 'The Elenchic Method'. One thing that's great about it is that anyone old enough and with normal wits and mind can use it and make at least some headway. The Elenchic Method is as good for philosophy as wiper fluid is for the front window of an automobile. What else is so great about this simple matter of asking whether or not one knows what 'good' is, is that its cheap but still works even if you're rich. Whether hanging out in a slum or heading up the mountain on a ski lift at a resort in the Alps, The Elenchic Method will still work.

Training in logic and critical thinking are the best mental supports for the Elenchic Method. Using it while drunk or in a rage will not yield the best results, but that isn't because it is crap.

Conclusions and personal knowledge/belief

Well, readers are not expected to all agree with the author at all times. However, in order to be clear, it is probably better to just write to you what I really think. I think that good and evil, right and wrong are real. I don't think humans invented them. I do think the Judeo-Christian story about 'the Fall' of Adam and Eve from eating fruit from the Tree of Knowledge tells us about the relationship between nature and morality. Human kind learns right and wrong by accumulating knowledge. They were real the whole time, but the ignorance of innocence of Adam & Eve before the Fall is like the innocence of babies.

Knowing the difference does cause the sense of pain associated with the transformation from conceiving of activities without moral considerations over to looking at them with an ethical attitude. Now they know, and because they know, they have the ability to feel guilt and regret and sorrow—which are all unpleasant emotions.

In truth, the author's limited perception is that good and evil and right and wrong really are there. A lot of it we can learn. We suffer when we learn the hard way. We suffer when we're right but others teach or even try to force us to do what we know is wrong. We can help others see the truth and we can wreak havoc by trying to correct others—especially since the degree of our own patience may not always meet the circumstances well. I do think people can actually know right and wrong. I do think that when people have knowledge of right and wrong that these people do not 'merely believe' in 'what is right or wrong to them'. I think this applies to me and not only to me. I think that religions of the good and society often encourage a lot of the good. However, I think society and culture also creates a lot of problems for its own people whether by forcing people to work for bosses who have morality they don't agree with, or teaching obedience to bad leadership, or disobedience when offered good leadership. I think there will always be people who feel that getting drunk on Friday night after working all week is OK and that there will always be other people who think the most important thing is the religious worship.

That leaves a lot of open space as it is. The views given are the present summation of 20 years of introspection with 5 years of formal training in philosophy and another 10 years of contemplation and dabbling and religious practice 'when not in an academic atmosphere'. For those interested there are vast tomes of knowledge about every aspect of this discussion. There is enough for every reader to make a career out of just a small portion of this. Please receive these conclusions with the awareness that this is the concise summary based on a lot which cannot be shown here.

Chapter 5: What is the Best Way to Live?

This is another of the most famous and important philosophical questions which exists. In fact, some of the different types of philosophers can be organized according to which of the Big 5 Questions that they answer and deal with.

This one involves some of the most intense personal practice that anyone can do. For hands on people who like to take action, dealing with this question is very fulfilling. One looks around and see that there is more than one way to live. People live differently for a variety of reasons. Some of the reasons involve matters we have control over and other factors are beyond our control.

The best way to live is normally influenced by what natural and social forces seem to govern. Our gender, our age and our cultural identity all influence how we view the world, what our needs and expectations are and how we operate. Within the limitations placed upon us by those factors most of us find that we still have some room to maneuver—there is some element of choice somewhere in our life.

Both religion and politics are involved here. Some people are born in nations where they have the free choice to move to many of the other countries in the world. Others are not. For those that do have that freedom, then they may choose where to live in part based upon which type of politics they prefer. They may select a place where they feel they the best economic chances. They may choose their preferred climate.

Religions of the good, and many of the political systems of the world teach that we are all improved by helping others. There are philosophies that advocate selfishness: some are openly evil whereas others are not intended to be evil at all but rather argue that the dignity and human and civil rights of people means that it is okay to be selfish—at least as far as refusing to be abused by political, religious or even familial systems—healthy selfishness is defined completely by the philosopheress Ayn Rand. Objectivism explains that people do not deserve or need to be suckered into being sacrificed to a system. One's personal well being and preferences are important.

What is the best way to live? This could also be called 'lifestyle philosophy'. One of the other most important elements that most Americans are familiar with is the scale of indulgence. There are extremes of indulgence—hedonism in known as the end of spectrum that indulges in pleasures and thinks that more pleasure is generally better. The other extreme is asceticism—these people normally claim that getting overly involved with either pleasure or pain is a bad idea and a distraction from what matters most. Upon inspection, especially to those coming from a more hedonistic standpoint—the ascetics take 'going without' to extremes.

One mild form of ascetism is the 'simple living' movement, or voluntary poverty where the people stay away from accumulating a lot of material goods and property, viewing such things as more of a burden and a vulnerability to be tricked into unethical behaviors.

Every individual has a life and is faced with how much or little control over it there is. Then there is the real task of assessing the options that are available to one. Given what they actually are, one needs to become aware of what one believes and of how one actually behaves. Sometimes, what one believes and the way one behaves are united. This in itself is a considerable achievement. That statement is a claim. I am claiming that it is valuable to live—to act in the world, according to the beliefs one has. This is a claim that part of the best way to live, is to live what one believes. This is not 'just me'. Jesus Christ is known to have taught this.

There are counter arguments to that. If one's actual beliefs would get one into terrible trouble in the society in which one lives and one cannot leave it, then perhaps it is best to live according to some leader's beliefs instead. This could be argued for politics, religion, state or federal governments and sometimes even in peer groups or families and also corporations and schools.

Another counter argument might be that people's beliefs can change, and since that would affect the whole lifestyle, maybe its not a good idea to live by a changing set. A completely different type of counter argument is that: one's beliefs are not really what runs the daily operations of one's life. This is more the type of thinking that secular society allows people who have differing beliefs to function together as part of the same basic society.

Culture

Living in a culture has a huge effect on every individual. Everyone knows this and yet, one's culture is so much a part of who one is, that most people don't really think about it. When people confront a different culture it becomes more noticeable.

Answering the question 'What is the best way to live?' involves culture. Every society has its norms, the dominant ways and the subdominant ways that are still strong enough that they are well known as 'subcultures' in any country. The main customs—but also both the politics and religious practices of a location can determine how one is going to express their choices. In the most extreme cases of a very bad match, a person may be able to actually leave a country or a town and go someplace else. In reality this happens fairly often. Sometimes people relocate just to meet new people so they can 'try again' and recreate their identities or change some of their ways.

Here, of course, it helps to know one's preferences. Self-knowledge is a treasure. Most people have it, but awareness about that can vary.

People are encouraged to live in accordance with their preferences but there is a limit to this. The limit involves morality—see the previous chapter. Anyone who suffers from behavior patterns or tendencies that go against the grain of good ethics should not simply 'do as they like' but rather, should seek conditions that allow them to nurture their better behavior and to quell the activity of their problem areas.

Naturally, one area of conflict for people can be a difference in one's true beliefs and the local culture. Most societies also offer various paths, that go along with the aspects of morality and preferences amongst human populations. This can make finding one's way more challenging—when there is the need to avoid trouble, but also offers some hope—even if one is rather unusual, one can still fit in and be acceptable and find people with whom one can relate well. Obviously, quirks are not uncommon.

There are people who believe that the best way to live is dictated by religion; some believe God has set out the ground rules and these need to be followed if there is to be any hope of real happiness. Other people feel that taking a more natural route is better. Those who are aware of how much is involved in raising humans probably know about some mistakes but also how much is gained through all the education. Its hard to say what people might be like if any survived to adulthood without being raised. Most wild animals teach their young a number of things, but humans learn even more.

The Individual

People get to be individuals. In the USA and in Christian cultures this is highly valued. The best way for a given person to live is closely tied up with highly valuing the life and qualities of each individual. Families and schools both attempt to nurture this, with varying degrees of success.

There are limits to this 'individual freedom'; the limits of the law are not meant to crush the spirit of individuals but are meant to protect the society at large from individuals whose idea of personal liberty includes trampling upon the wills of others in the same society. That's the best truthful interpretation of this. Religions, and the law of the land contribute to setting limits on individual freedom but solely for the sake of protecting each member of the society from overrunning the others.

For the purpose of this project, we will not go into abuses of the use of law or corruption of governments. While those are real concerns, that is not the limit and purpose of laws. The main philosophy of the Western tradition that deals with this, is John Stuart Mill's famous "utilitarianism."

Adults especially are duty bound to serve the society. The laws that limit personal freedom are made to serve the total population. This does mean that people may not just do whatever they feel like to one another. Even so, the idea is to establish a morally good atmosphere that assures the relative safety and protection of all members of the society.

Children constitute a special class of people. Although they are not full citizens they are expected to be once they grow up. To a limited degree women continue to be a somewhat different category from the men of the society. This is largely due to tendencies towards care in families, distribution of labor, and the economic limitations: fixed numbers of jobs, and the need to share resources. Marriage is largely a means by which to ensure the safety of women and children—that they will be included in the material resources of a given man. While many women do work and increasing proportions earn enough to support themselves and children, as well as having the rights of citizenship in numerous nations including the USA, women still function a bit differently from the men, and differently from the children. All of these 'limits' are meant to create an ethical atmosphere and are not intended to be to the detriment of individuals.

Society

A society can be viewed as if it were an organism or entity although it is a level of organization. These can be made to be oriented more or less towards 'the good, the just and the beautiful' or not. They may be founded upon certain ideas or ideals. Most nations have slogans and oaths of some kind which give at least some clue regarding what they are about. Of course, one needs to either know the language or have a translation in order to get the message. This is one of those things: people generally know what one is, but don't think about it that much.

Societies are made up of individuals, institutions—only one of which is 'the government', informal organizations, customs and 'history' or 'tradition'. The real key for this discussion is to see how they fit together. There is an old saying "It is difficult to see the forest for the trees, or 'I can't see the trees because of the forest'." Mainly, this shows how much we are affected by the level of organization we see something from. The individual in society taken on the whole, is typically invisible.

Fame, means that even though it is an individual or small group of people the entire society actually knows who that is, or huge portions of the population actually know who that is. Unlike the famous, the vast majority of individuals remains invisible on the mass scale, but is important to smaller numbers of people. In some cases, there is even a relationship between the two: people who are so devoted to a small number of people that they give all of their energy to that group are not noticed. Others give their energy to hordes of people and sometimes find that hardly anyone is able to be around them often and to go into depth in a decidedly personal way.

The majority of people lives between these extremes but actually tend more towards the small group focus. Some of their energy goes to the famous, and some goes to other levels of the society in which they dwell and most of it stays with families and friends. The reason 'families' is used here is to include both the parents and people one grows up with and also spouses and offspring, or any other highly relevant people.

Societies need to have vision and direction. Many factors combine to give them unique identities. Religion, government, culture—language, customs, religious attitudes and practices are defining features. Modes of production—how the people are fed, what the society makes, what technology they have and how it is applied, and what is exported and to whom also play into the identity of a society.

Individuals somehow have to make their way in society. There are people who really like the society into which they are born and others who feel as if they don't really fit in. Some who don't fit in, leave and discover joyfully that they fit in better someplace else. Others learn to fit in. There are those who are 'themselves' and those who get by using varying degrees of deception and secrecy just to keep others from persecuting them.

In this case, 'fitting in' is used rather loosely. Everyone who is able to stay out of prison and usually uninjured, free from persecution and able to earn or to receive enough funding to not be impoverished is 'fitting in' well enough. This is not the same degree of conformity as being the status quo or being the most popular person in a clique. Every society has 'outsiders' and 'misfits' and 'odd balls' in addition to 'criminals' 'villains' and 'the stigmatized.'

People are typically taught a great deal about how to fit in by being raised and educated within a culture. There are limits to it:

gender and social class are both major cultural forces, aside from religion which shape people's views of the world and the perception of 'what is right' in dealing with some of life's issues and challenges. The training can help in many situations but there are also times when the social conditioning can cause trouble for a person—especially if there is an unusual drive in that individual—towards behaviors better suited to some other social class or to what the majority view as belonging to the other gender. In such situations, the whole and practice of unconventional living surfaces like a submarine in the ocean. Now there's a reason for a person to pursue 'being different' while still needing to 'fit into society' at the same time.

Cultures also react to this differently. Not every nation is the same way about individuality and its expression, and there may be special options and alternatives available to people within a given subculture. Human civilization is sometimes almost comical in terms of being 'the same but different.'

Globalization in some ways suppresses cultural differences terribly but in other ways it fosters more diversity. Each culture has some unique methods for people to be nonconformists without making themselves socially unacceptable—in general terms, in the USA at least, these often function as well known subcultures.

Essentially society and the individual are largely mutually dependent. In truth, human adults who know how can survive in the wild without other people but they would have to go without cars and knives let alone designer purses and good doctors. Human children cannot survive their first years without the help of adults. The wildest exceptions ever heard of involve adults of some animal species successfully caring for a human infant—on their own they just won't make it.

Often enough, in the 21st century humans in many parts of the world do not feel there is any longer any choice about whether or not to live within society. One must. There are still some places and some people for whom this is a choice, but often it is more true than false that the option for a human adult to live in the wild is gone from our Earth. Given that limitation, few people, if any still have perspective about whether or not one lifestyle is truly preferable. It is possible that the vast majority prefer civilization—if only for the medical care and the schools and the shopping malls but there is a general social malaise which often seems to be caused by the loss of living free and wild as a real option. Rumor has it that for those who really know how, life in the wild is not that bad. In fact, rumor has it that humans can be happy that way although by the civilized view they would probably all be poor and unemployed and largely illiterate people. Many of them also die young; around 40, or during childhood.

Given that, then in general the need to 'fit in' is intense. It is related to survival needs. For many, the struggle on the surface is not one of survival but is a question of whether or not one can own a home, have an in ground swimming pool and send the kids to private or public schools. For some reason, the emotions and reactions that people experience often make things like this seem as if they are on the same level as survival needs even though they are obviously not.

The nature of the society any individual finds himself or herself in will strongly influence the individuality and the expression of that. There are cultures where "I" is viewed as a bad thing or as an illusion and other cultures where "I" is viewed as healthy, real and to be celebrated not squelched.

The biggest reason that caste systems were rebelled against in many nations was the idea that there are people who are born into a caste other than the one they are best suited to. People should have at least some chance to move from one to another. Although this conflict was made most infamous by India, European nations and the USA all do have such issues, but they call them 'class' rather than 'caste.'

What is the best way to live?

Here the theory of: what is the best way to live? Is simply to be oneself, to be a good person and to behave in a way that one's individuality is enhanced through service to the society one lives in. On the same line of thinking: the individuality of a person, rather than being any detriment, helps to dictate to that individual, what the best way to fit in and to contribute is.

The need to contribute to the society in which one lives comes at individuals through both secular and religious directions. In reality, it has to do with taking a share of responsibility for maintaining the society which has provided one with a society during childhood. This is why in some respects, there can be a problem with people moving around—in that, it means one has left the realm that gave to one, and is giving elsewhere. In some locations this is balanced out and is not a real problem, but most readers will have heard of 'brain drain' and that's a sign that the system is out of balance. A place is nurturing people but then losing them and isn't receiving a balancing force.

With this as a context: whenever anyone answers the question of the best way to live, they can and have to, take into account what society they are really living in when they do it. This is as important as taking into account one's individuality. In the worst cases, one has to either leave, or change the society or change oneself considerably if there is any hope of functioning well there.

The ideal is in fact this: that the individuality of a person fits perfectly into the society in a natural but well disciplined way and both the society and the individual benefit. This produces happy people—or at least helps.

Much of the pains and sufferings of adults—are not physical injuries at all but are all about people trying to manage situations that don't fit them that well and how to either adjust to the circumstances or else change the conditions the individual is dealing with. This also occurs for kids and it also happens for groups but it is significant.

There are many factors which help this and others which cause trouble for individuals or for the societies of which they are a part. Although this theory is relatively simple, implementation often requires the vast majority of the effort

Control

When people make efforts to deal with life and to be happy people there are two main loci of control to help do this: events and the self. Events include everything external—money, other people, and environment—all of it.

The self includes everything from physical fitness, fashion and cosmetics, religion, the mind—learning or meditations or prayers or dance lessons and psychotherapy. All of those things. One of the most important requisites for implementing anything is control.

Figuring out how much control one has over what factors and features of one's life is part of the process. People naturally find out about how much or little control they have while they grow up. Often, new stages of life are seen as 'game changers'; adults have different limitations than teens than little kids.

Career or 'the calling'

One major factor during the adult life about determining 'the best way to live' involves funding. One must have funding or be able to receive resources directly. The situation for men and women really is still different: men are more likely to experience pressure to provide for children and any mother/s of offspring whereas woman are more liable to experience the need to let themselves be dependent upon their offspring's father or some other man in a private relationship while they tend to babies. More women are spending more energy earning money during the past two centuries—at least in the middle class: poor women have always had to work, but it might not have been the way one might imagine it. She was probably at the spinning wheel—which would make binding the baby so it doesn't wiggle into danger handy. Even so, more women were able to go without paying work and forced to go without paying work than men.

In reality, for women more than men one big question that must be faced when asking what one's calling or career path is: is it doing the full time 'career mother' or is it actually something else? For some the answer is motherhood. For others the answer is really a specific career. That doesn't cover everyone: many women may discover something relatively in between the extreme of work or maternity, marriage or a career. Many women, especially amongst the upper classes, had partial careers doing volunteer social service. While easily overlooked, they really provided a great deal of precious effort—often on behalf of poorer people who either could not afford to go without the pay to do what they did, or who did not really have the generosity of spirit or education necessary to do the jobs they did. So, for women more than for men: there is a real need to look at the whole of life to find what major activities are the best ways for one to express one's unique and best qualities.

For men, in general, the answer is more likely to involve paying work since being paid helps them provide for themselves and also entire families and children while also enforcing the need to serve the common good. This does not mean that the work life is always the key for a man, but it is more likely to be so than for women.

The type of work a man does is his calling if he finds it fulfilling and has an inborn 'knack' or talent and interest in doing it. This can be auspiciously benefited by one's social position— one might be born into a family that has people who will support the right conditions for one to move into the best possible line of work. Those who have this situation are fortunate.

Others may find themselves faced with the opposite: that they are born into an environment which will interfere with them finding the best line of work because their parents or social class may expect and pressure them to do something else. For such people working through that challenge may be a major part of their lives until they work it out and manage to get to 'their calling'.

In truth, I believe that there are people for whom there is no 'calling' or ideal career, and I think some of the people this happens to are men but more are women. This makes decisions about work rather different. One could spend a good chunk of time seeking to find one's best career when really there is no 'right answer' for that individual, or there are so many best answers that it may seem as if it doesn't even matter. Somehow, this type of person needs to realize that and then make decisions based upon other dominant features of their identity—taking into account the needs of the society in which they dwell.

While work is not the be all, end all of life—what one does for work and how much one works is intimately related to responding to the question of the best way to live. One needs to be able to figure out what it is, and how to implement it within the limits of their actual situation.

Religion

Religion is often part of the answer to the best way to live. The purpose behind much of it is to offer people a supportive environment in which to be good people or to work to become better and grow more mature in a safe place. This includes spiritual nourishment. There are a variety of religions but the main choice is typically provided by one's nation as a 'strong and guided suggestion'.

For some folks, involvement with religion is counter-productive and for them, part of the best life is about not even practicing a religion. Personally I do believe there may be some people for whom this is true but I believe that more than 80% of the population is better off having and practicing a religion. The truth might be closer to 99% than to 80, but I'm not absolutely certain about it.

Love Style

People do best with love in their lives. How people experience this and express their affections over the course of the lifetime is another important aspect of 'what the best way to live' really is for a given individual.

There are normally multiple types of love in a person's life, most are not directly sexual, but there may be elements of indirect sexuality—in the form of children being an indirect form of their parents' sexual activity, or friendships that are motivated by attraction but never turn into romances or sexual activity.

Sexual love, romance, a sense of the morality surrounding those involved and any children who show up is also a very major and important part of people practicing their best way to live. People need to be safe: traditional forms of family; represented by marriage, is one of the best ways for people to be safe to have sex. Like it or not, this is a truth.

Not everyone is identical and there may be some variations, but essentially, making sure that anyone and everyone involved has sufficient material provisions and is treated with love and respect and any emerging children are either given to people who will take good care of them or kept by people who will love them and be able to provide for them. This is a clear moral / ethical viewpoint. Personally, I believe that the pleasures, the reproduction and the intensity of associated interaction caused involved with sexual activity are spiritual in nature. People can, through their choices, make sex a sacred and beautiful, wholesome activity or can degrade the inherent spiritual nature of it.

Most of the love relationships are not of that type and may involve other relations that range from deeply personal—families and friends, to more abstract: organizations, the local school board or the church congregation or Amnesty International or what have you, or a petroleum corporation or public park and associated committees.

For all of these relationships, every person has the opportunity to express their individuality through and in conjunction with social activity. Over the course of a lifetime, all of these things taken together make up a person's love style.

CPSIA information can be obtained at www.ICGtesting.com
Printed in the USA
LVOW13s0104301113

363195LV00005B/13/P

9 781617 208645